Turnstiles

Turn strips of different shades of one color into lovely pinwheels in this quick and easy quilt.

Design by Gina Gempesaw
Quilted by Carole Whaling

Skill Level
Confident Beginner

Finished Size
Quilt Size: 53¾" x 53¾"
Block Size: 13¼" x 13¼" finished
Number of Blocks: 9

Materials
- ⅓ yard light teal check
- 1⅛ yards medium teal print
- 1½ yards dark teal tonal
- 2⅛ yards white/teal print
- Backing to size
- Batting to size
- Thread
- Basic sewing tools and supplies

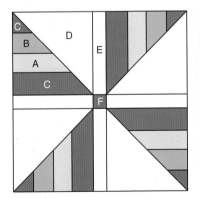

Turnstile A
13¼" x 13¼" Finished Block
Make 5

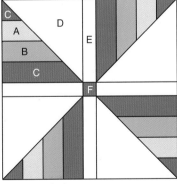

Turnstile AR
13¼" x 13¼" Finished Block
Make 4

Project Notes

Read all instructions before beginning this project. Stitch right sides together using a ¼" seam allowance unless otherwise specified. Refer to a favorite quilting guide for specific techniques. Materials and cutting lists assume 40" of usable fabric width.

Cutting

From light teal check:
- Cut 4 (2" by fabric width) A strips.

From medium teal print:
- Cut 4 (2" by fabric width) B strips.
- Cut 6 (3½" by fabric width) K/L strips.

From dark teal tonal:
- Cut 8 (2¼" by fabric width) C strips.
- Cut 6 (1½" by fabric width) strips.
  Subcut 1 strip into 25 (1½") F squares. Set aside remaining strips for I/J strips.
- Cut 6 (2¼" by fabric width) binding strips.

From white/teal print:
- Cut 4 (7" by fabric width) strips.
  Subcut strips into 18 (7") squares. Cut each square in half on 1 diagonal to make 36 D triangles.
- Cut 3 (6⅝" by fabric width) strips.
  Subcut strips into 60 (1½" x 6⅝") E strips.
- Cut 5 (2½" by fabric width) G/H strips.

Completing the Blocks

1. Sew an A strip to a B strip and add a C strip to the A and B sides to make a strip set as shown in Figure 1. Press seams in one direction. Repeat to make a total of four strip sets.

Make 4

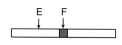

Figure 1

2. Subcut the strip sets into 20 (7") squares as shown in Figure 2.

Cut 20
7"

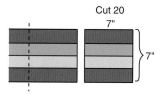

Figure 2

3. Cut each square in half on one diagonal to make 20 each A and AR triangles as shown in Figure 3. Set aside four AR triangles for another project.

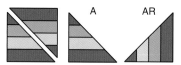

A   AR

Figure 3

4. Sew each A and AR triangle to a D triangle to make 20 A-D units and 16 AR-D units as shown in Figure 4; press seams toward D.

A-D Unit   AR-D Unit
Make 20   Make 16

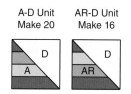

Figure 4

5. To complete one Turnstile A block, select four each A-D units and E strips, and one F square.

6. Join two A-D units with an E strip to make an A-D-E row as shown in Figure 5; press. Repeat to make a second A-D-E row.

Make 2

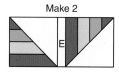

Figure 5

7. Join two E strips with one F square to make the center row as shown in Figure 6; press.

E   F

Figure 6

Introduction

Pretty Pinwheels is a collection of fabulous quilts all created with pinwheel blocks. This book takes the traditional pinwheel to new and exciting places. You'll never think of pinwheels the same way once you page through this book. You'll find pinwheels made with Drunkard's Path units, striped piecing, paper piecing, with appliqué embellishments and so much more. *Pretty Pinwheels* will open the door to your imagination and give you permission to explore other possibilities.

Skill levels range from confident beginner to intermediate and projects vary from wall hangings to bed-size quilts. As an added value and more options, we've added extra layout diagrams for those who would like to change the designer's original size. There's something for creative quilters and inspiration for all. Pinwheels will never seem the same once you discover *Pretty Pinwheels*.

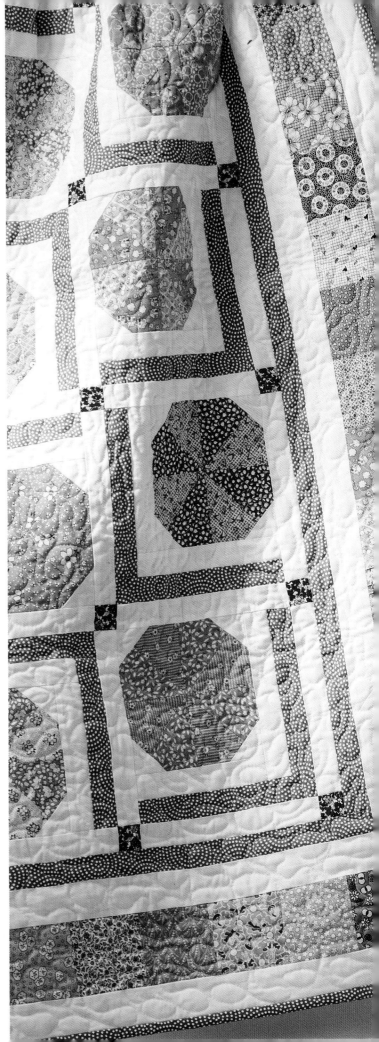

Table of Contents

8. Join the two A-D-E rows with the center row to complete one Turnstile A block as shown in Figure 7; press.

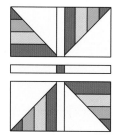

Figure 7

9. Repeat steps 5–8 to complete a total of five Turnstile A blocks.

10. Repeat steps 5–8 with the AR-D units to complete a total of four Turnstile AR blocks referring to Figure 8.

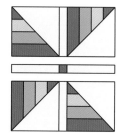

Figure 8

Completing the Quilt Top
Refer to the Assembly Diagram for positioning of blocks, sashing and borders.

1. Sew an F square between two E strips to make a sashing unit, again referring to Figure 6; press. Repeat to make a total of 12 sashing units.

2. Arrange and join two Turnstile A blocks with one Turnstile AR block and two sashing units to make the top row; press. Repeat to make the bottom row.

3. Arrange and join two Turnstile AR blocks with one Turnstile A block and two sashing units to make the center row; press.

4. Arrange and join three sashing units and two F squares to make a sashing row; press. Repeat to make a second sashing row.

5. Join the block rows and the sashing rows to complete the quilt center; press.

6. Join the G/H strips on the short ends to make a long strip; press. Subcut strip into two each 2½" x 42¼" G strips and 2½" x 46¼" H strips.

7. Sew G strips to the top and bottom and H strips to opposite sides of the quilt center; press.

8. Join the I/J strips on the short ends to make a long strip; press. Subcut strip into two each 1½" x 46¼" I strips and 1½" x 48¼" J strips.

9. Sew I strips to the top and bottom and J strips to opposite sides of the quilt center; press.

10. Join the K/L strips on the short ends to make a long strip; press. Subcut strip into two each 3½" x 48¼" K strips and 3½" x 56¼" L strips.

11. Sew K strips to the top and bottom and L strips to opposite sides of the quilt center to complete the quilt top; press.

12. Layer, quilt and bind referring to Quilting Basics on page 60 to finish. ●

Inspiration

"Going through subway turnstiles inspired this quilt." —Gina Gempesaw

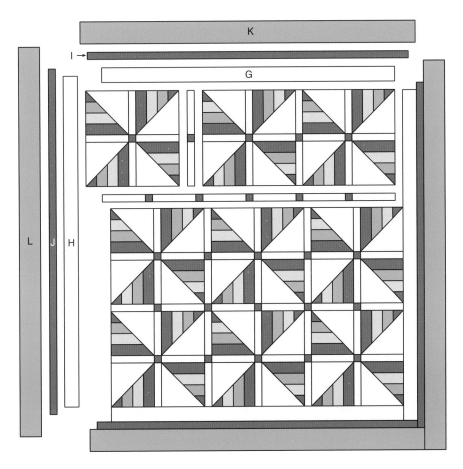

Turnstiles
Assembly Diagram 53³/₄" x 53³/₄"

Pinwheel Baby

Turn Drunkard's Path units into pretty pinwheels that will work wonders with any fun collection. This quilt is destined to become Baby's favorite.

Designed & Quilted by Tricia Lynn Maloney

Skill Level
Intermediate

Finished Size
Quilt Size: 45" x 45"
Block Sizes: 9" x 9" finished
Number of Blocks: 12

Materials
- ¼ yard each mint, taupe, orange 1, orange 2 and gray prints
- ⅜ yard yellow print
- ½ yard gray/yellow print
- ⅞ yard white print
- ⅞ yard yellow animal print
- Backing to size
- Batting to size
- Thread
- Template material
- Basic sewing tools and supplies

Project Notes
Read all instructions before beginning this project. Stitch right sides together using a ¼" seam allowance unless otherwise specified. Refer to a favorite quilting guide for specific techniques. Materials and cutting lists assume 40" of usable fabric width.

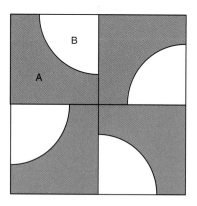

Drunkard's Pinwheel
9" x 9" Finished Block
Make 12

Cutting
Prepare template for A and B pieces using patterns given on insert; cut from strips as directed below and/or on patterns.

From mint, taupe, orange 1, orange 2 & gray prints:
- Cut 1 (5" by fabric width) strip each fabric.
  Subcut mint, taupe, orange 1 and gray strips into 8 A pieces each and orange 2 strip into 4 A pieces using the A template on the strips.

From yellow print:
- Cut 2 (5" by fabric width) strips.
  Subcut strips into 12 A pieces using the A template on the strips.

From gray/yellow print:
- Cut 5 (2¼" by fabric width) binding strips.

From white print:
- Cut 5 (3½" by fabric width) strips. Subcut strips into 48 B pieces using the B template on the strips.
- Cut 2 (5" x 36½") C strips.

From yellow animal print:
- Cut 2 (5" x 36½") D strips.
- Cut 3 (5" by fabric width) E strips.

Completing the Blocks

1. Matching center points, sew a B piece to an A piece to make a total of 48 A-B units referring to Figure 1. ***Note:*** *Use your favorite curved-piecing technique or refer to Curved Piecing on page 12.*

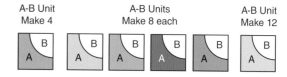

Figure 1

2. Select four matching A-B units and join to make two rows of two units each as shown in Figure 2; press.

Figure 2

3. Join the rows as shown in Figure 3 to complete one Drunkard's Pinwheel block; press.

Figure 3

4. Repeat steps 2 and 3 to complete a total of 12 Drunkard's Pinwheel blocks.

Completing the Quilt Top

Refer to the Assembly Diagram for positioning of blocks, strips and borders.

1. Arrange and join four Drunkard's Pinwheel blocks to make a vertical block row; press. Repeat to make a total of three rows.

2. Join the block rows with the C strips to complete the quilt center; press seams toward the strips.

3. Sew D strips to opposite sides of the quilt center; press seams toward D.

4. Join the E strips on the short ends to make a long strip; press. Subcut strip into two 5" x 45½" E strips.

5. Sew an E strip to the top and bottom of the quilt center to complete the quilt top; press seams toward E.

6. Layer, quilt and bind referring to Quilting Basics on page 60 to finish. ●

Inspiration

"I have always been fascinated by the different designs that can be created using a simple Drunkard's Path unit." —Tricia Lynn Maloney

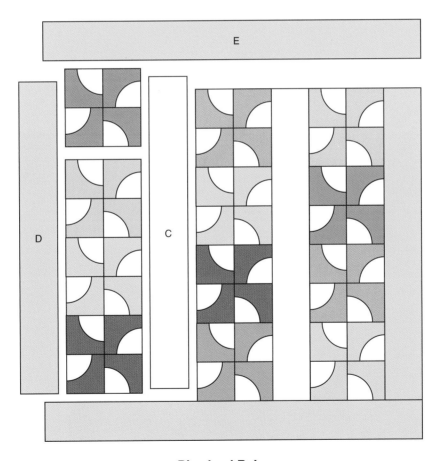

Pinwheel Baby
Assembly Diagram 45" x 45"

Curved Piecing

There are many traditional quilt blocks and free-form designs that use curves. Like many other quilting techniques, a few tips and a little practice will make curved piecing less of a struggle and open up your design choices.

Careful cutting and marking of curved pieces is critical to having a smooth curved seam. Curved seams are bias edges and will stretch easily without careful handling.

Curves With Templates

Make templates from template plastic or freezer paper for traditional blocks. You can also purchase acrylic templates for most common curved shapes in different sizes. Or, use a die-cut system to cut multiple shapes accurately.

Be sure to follow the template as closely as possible when cutting pieces. If using a rotary blade, use the smallest rotary blade size available to easily negotiate the curves. If using scissors, move the fabric/template instead of the scissors when cutting. Be sure your scissors are sharp.

Find the centers of both the convex (outer curve) and concave (inner curve) edges by folding the pieces in half, finger-press and mark with a pin. Purchased templates and die-cut pieces should have center notches. Match the centers and pin with the convex curve on the top referring to the Drunkard's Path block in Figure A.

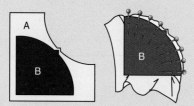

Figure A

Match and pin the seam ends. Then pin liberally between the seam ends and center, matching the seam edges and referring again to Figure A.

Slowly stitch pieces together an inch or two at a time, removing pins and keeping seam edges even.

Clip only the concave seam allowance if necessary. Press seam allowances flat toward the concave curve (Figure B).

Figure B

Common traditional blocks like Apple Core and Robbing Peter to Pay Paul are constructed in the same manner.

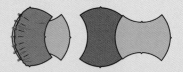

Apple Core

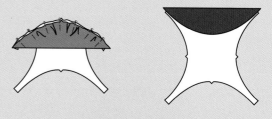

Robbing Peter to Pay Paul

Curves Without Templates

To make gentle curves without templates, overlap two pieces of fabric right sides up (Figure C1). Cut a gentle curve with a rotary cutter through both layers of fabric (Figure C2). Discard the fabric remnants (Figure C3). **Note:** You can cut a single curve as shown here or an undulating curve as shown in Figure D. Just keep the curves gentle and shallow.

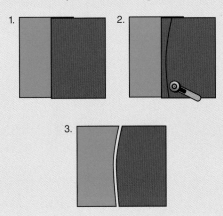

Figure C

For single or undulating curves, mark across the cut pieces with curved edges matching (Figure D). Make shallow clips in the concave areas referring again to Figure D.

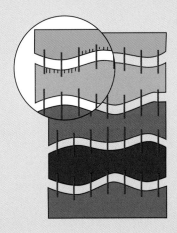

Figure D

Pin the curved edges together matching the marks (Figure E). Slowly stitch pieces together an inch or two at a time, removing pins and keeping seam edges even.

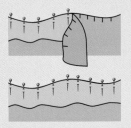

Figure E

Free-form quilters use single and undulating curves to add movement or a landscape feel to their quilts.

Single Curves

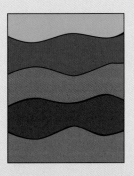

Undulating Curves

Candy Kisses

Choose two contrasting fabrics for each block for a double pinwheel look. Making this quilt is a great way to clean out your 1930s reproduction fabrics.

Designed & Quilted by Julie Weaver

Skill Level

Confident Beginner

Finished Size

Quilt Size: 51" x 60"
Block Size: 8" x 8" finished
Number of Blocks: 20

Materials

- 20 different 4" x 8" A rectangles reproduction prints
- 20 different 4" x 8" B rectangles reproduction prints
- 66 (3½") N squares variety of reproduction prints
- ⅛ yard red print
- 1⅜ yards blue-and-white print
- 2⅛ yards white solid
- Backing to size
- Batting to size
- Thread
- Basic sewing tools and supplies

Project Notes

Read all instructions before beginning this project. Stitch right sides together using a ¼" seam allowance unless otherwise specified. Refer to a favorite quilting guide for specific techniques. Materials and cutting lists assume 40" of usable fabric width.

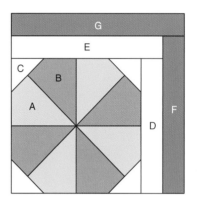

Candy Kiss
8" x 8" Finished Block
Make 20

Cutting

From A & B rectangles:

- Cut 2 (3⅞") squares from each rectangle to total 40 each A and B squares.

From red print:

- Cut 2 (1½" by fabric width) strips.
  Subcut strips into 30 (1½") I squares.

From blue-and-white print:

- Cut 1 (7½" by fabric width) strip.
  Subcut strip into 20 (1½" x 7½") F strips.
- Cut 1 (8½" by fabric width) strip.
  Subcut strip into 20 (1½" x 8½") G strips.
- Cut 5 (1½" by fabric width) J/K strips.
  Trim 2 strips to make 2 (1½" x 39½") K strips.
  Set aside remaining strips for J.
- Cut 6 (2¼" by fabric width) binding strips.

From white solid:
- Cut 4 (2" by fabric width) strips.
  Subcut strips into 80 (2") C squares.
- Cut 1 (6½" by fabric width) strip.
  Subcut strip into 20 (1½" x 6½") D strips.
- Cut 1 (7½" by fabric width) strip.
  Subcut strip into 20 (1½" x 7½") E strips.
- Cut 2 (8½" by fabric width) strips.
  Subcut strips into 49 (1½" x 8½") H strips.
- Cut 11 (2" by fabric width) L/M/O/P strips.

Here's a Tip

Control the scrappiness in this quilt by using just two prints for the pinwheel shapes in each block. Be sure you have enough contrast to make the pinwheel stand out.

Completing the Blocks

1. Draw a diagonal line from corner to corner on the wrong side of each A and C square.

2. To complete one Candy Kiss block, select two each matching A and matching B squares, four C squares and one each D, E, F and G strip.

3. Place an A square right sides together with a B square; stitch ¼" on each side of the marked line. Cut apart on the marked line and press open to make two A-B units as shown in Figure 1. Repeat with the second set of A and B squares to make two more units for a total of four A-B units.

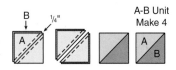

Figure 1

4. Join two A-B units to make a row as shown in Figure 2; press. Repeat to make a second row. **_Note:_** *See Spinning Centers to Reduce Bulk on page 20 for pressing center seams.*

Make 2

Figure 2

5. Join the rows as shown in Figure 3; press.

Figure 3

6. Place a marked C square right sides together on each corner of the pieced unit and stitch on the marked lines as shown in Figure 4. Trim excess seam allowance to ¼" and press C to the right side to complete one pinwheel unit, again referring to Figure 4.

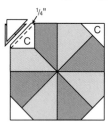

Figure 4

7. Sew D strip to the right edge of the pinwheel unit and E strip to the top; press. Repeat with F and G strips to complete one Candy Kiss block (Figure 5).

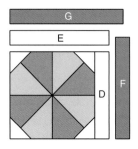

Figure 5

8. Repeat steps 2–7 to complete a total of 20 Candy Kiss blocks.

Completing the Quilt Top

Refer to the Assembly Diagram for positioning of blocks, sashing and borders.

1. Join four blocks and five H strips to make an A row as shown in Figure 6; press. Repeat to make a total of three A rows.

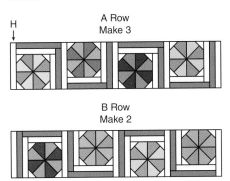

Figure 6

2. Repeat step 1 to make two B rows, again referring to Figure 6.

3. Join four H strips with five I squares to make a sashing row; press. Repeat to make a total of six sashing rows.

4. Join the A and B block rows and the sashing rows to complete the quilt center; press.

5. Join the J strips on the short ends to make a long strip; press. Subcut strip into two 1½" x 46½" J strips.

6. Sew the J strips to opposite long sides and K strips to the top and bottom of the quilt center; press.

7. Join the L/M/O/P strips on the short ends to make a long strip; press. Subcut strip into two each 2" x 48½" L strips, 2" x 42½" M strips, 2" x 57½" O strips and 2" x 51½" P strips.

8. Sew the L strips to opposite long sides and M strips to the top and bottom of the quilt center; press.

9. Join 17 N squares to make a pieced side strip; repeat to make a second strip. Press strips. Sew these strips to opposite long sides of the quilt center; press.

10. Repeat step 9 with 16 N squares to make two strips. Sew these strips to the top and bottom of the quilt center; press.

11. Sew O strips to opposite long sides and P strips to the top and bottom of the quilt center to complete the quilt top; press.

12. Layer, quilt and bind referring to Quilting Basics on page 60 to finish. ●

Candy Kisses
Assembly Diagram 51" x 60"

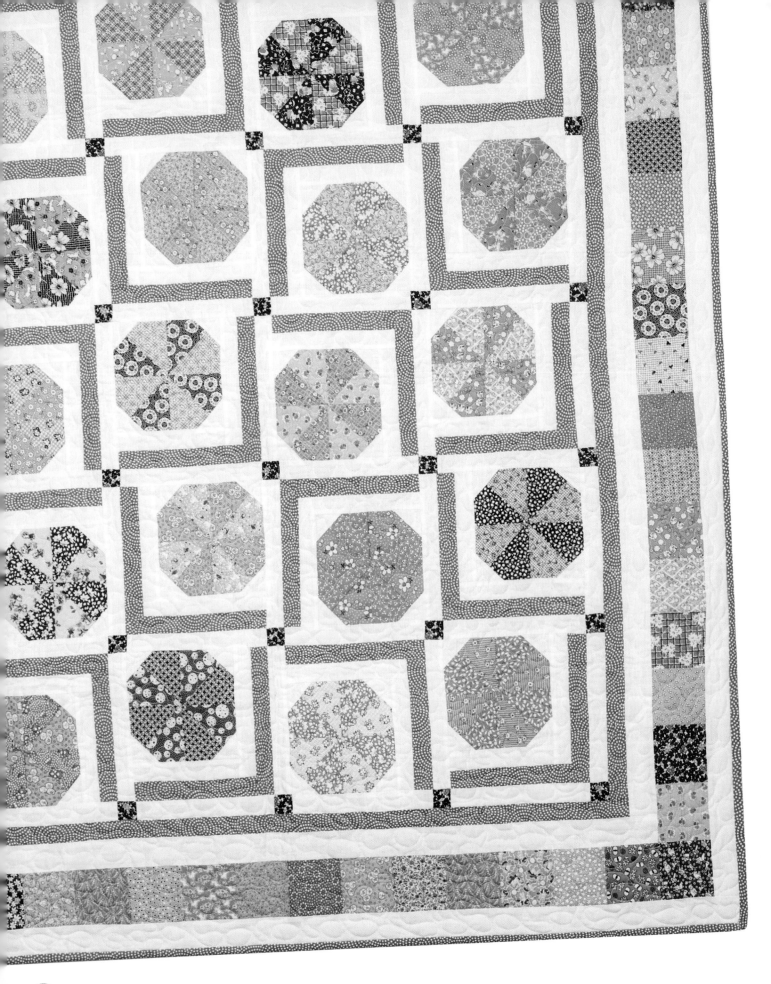

Inspiration

"The title of this book—Pretty Pinwheels—provided all the inspiration I needed for this quilt! Pinwheels and 1930s reproduction prints—they just seem to go together! I've been collecting these prints for many years, so I take any chance I can get to use some of them. It took me a while to warm up to these reproduction prints, but once I did, I was hooked." —Julie Weaver

Candy Kisses
Alternate Assembly Diagram 69" x 96"
Add 2 blocks to the width and 4 rows to the length to make a twin-size quilt.

Spinning Centers to Reduce Bulk

When sewing a block where numerous points meet together, there can be a lot of "bulk" in the seam allowance on the wrong side of the fabric. This extra bulk prohibits the block from lying flat when pressed. One option is to trim the points off thus reducing the amount of fabric in the seam allowance. Another option is to "spin" the center of the seam allowances thus distributing the bulk more evenly.

1. Stitch the block as usual nesting seams at any intersection (Photo A).

Photo A

2. Before pressing, remove approximately three stitches in the seam allowance from each side of the previously sewn seams (Photo B).

Photo B

3. Place the block on a pressing board right side down (Photo C).

Photo C

4. With your finger, push the top seam to the right and the bottom seam to the left. This will result in the seam allowances spinning in a clockwise direction (Photo D).

Photo D

5. The center will pop open and the seam allowances will swirl around the center of the block (Photo E).

Photo E

6. Press with an iron to flatten the seam allowances in place (Photo F).

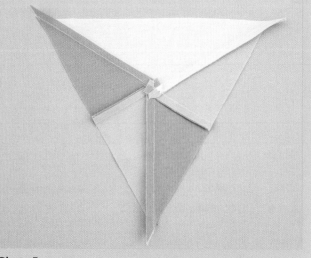

Photo F

Serenity

Pinwheel blocks in two sizes create an interesting setting when combined with current fabrics. The addition of several borders extends the design to give it a unique finished look.

Designed & Quilted by Julie Weaver

Skill Level

Confident Beginner

Finished Size

Quilt Size: 48" x 56"
Block Sizes: 8" x 8" finished
Number of Blocks: 20

Materials

- ⅝ yard gray tonal
- ¾ yard gray floral
- 1⅛ yards aqua floral
- 1¼ yards aqua tonal
- 1½ yards white solid
- Backing to size
- Batting to size
- Thread
- Basic sewing tools and supplies

Project Notes

Read all instructions before beginning this project. Stitch right sides together using a ¼" seam allowance unless otherwise specified. Refer to a favorite quilting guide for specific techniques. Materials and cutting lists assume 40" of usable fabric width.

Cutting

From gray tonal:

- Cut 1 (6½" by fabric width) strip.
  Subcut strip into 20 (1½" x 6½") G rectangles.
- Cut 1 (8½" by fabric width) strip.
  Subcut strip into 20 (1½" x 8½") H rectangles.

From gray floral:

- Cut 2 (3½" by fabric width) strips.
  Subcut strips into 40 (2" x 3½") D rectangles.
- Cut 5 (3" by fabric width) K/L strips.

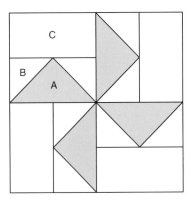

Pinwheel
8" x 8" Finished Block
Make 10

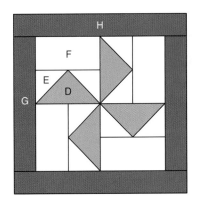

Framed Pinwheel
8" x 8" Finished Block
Make 10

From aqua floral:

- Cut 3 (4½" by fabric width) strips.
   Subcut strips into 40 (2½" x 4½") A rectangles.
- Cut 6 (3" by fabric width) O/P strips.

From aqua tonal:

- Cut 2 (2" x 35½") J strips.
- Cut 7 (2" by fabric width) I/M/N strips.
- Cut 6 (2¼" by fabric width) binding strips.

From white solid:

- Cut 5 (2½" by fabric width) strips.
   Subcut strips into 80 (2½") B squares.
- Cut 3 (4½" by fabric width) strips.
   Subcut strips into 40 (2½" x 4½") C rectangles.
- Cut 4 (2" by fabric width) strips.
   Subcut strips into 80 (2") E squares.
- Cut 2 (3½" by fabric width) strips.
   Subcut strips into 40 (2" x 3½") F rectangles.

Completing the Pinwheel Blocks

1. Refer to Three Ways to Make Flying Geese Units on page 27 to make 40 A-B units as shown in Figure 1.

A-B Unit
Make 40

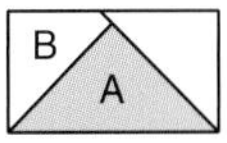

Figure 1

2. To complete one Pinwheel block, select four each A-B units and C rectangles.

3. Sew a C rectangle to an A-B unit to make a quarter unit as shown in Figure 2; press. Repeat to make a total of four quarter units.

Quarter Unit
Make 4

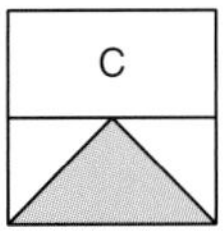

C

Figure 2

4. Join two quarter units to make a row; press. Repeat to make a second row. Join the rows to complete the block as shown in Figure 3.

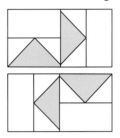

Figure 3

5. Repeat steps 2–4 to complete a total of 10 Pinwheel blocks.

Completing the Framed Pinwheel Blocks

1. Refer to Three Ways to Make Flying Geese Units on page 27 to make 40 D-E units as shown in Figure 4.

D-E Unit
Make 40

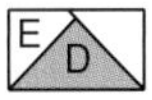

Figure 4

2. To complete one Framed Pinwheel block, select four each D-E units and F rectangles, and two each G and H rectangles.

3. Using D-E units and F rectangles, repeat steps 3 and 4 of Completing the Pinwheel Blocks to make the block center referring to Figure 5.

Block Center

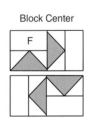

Figure 5

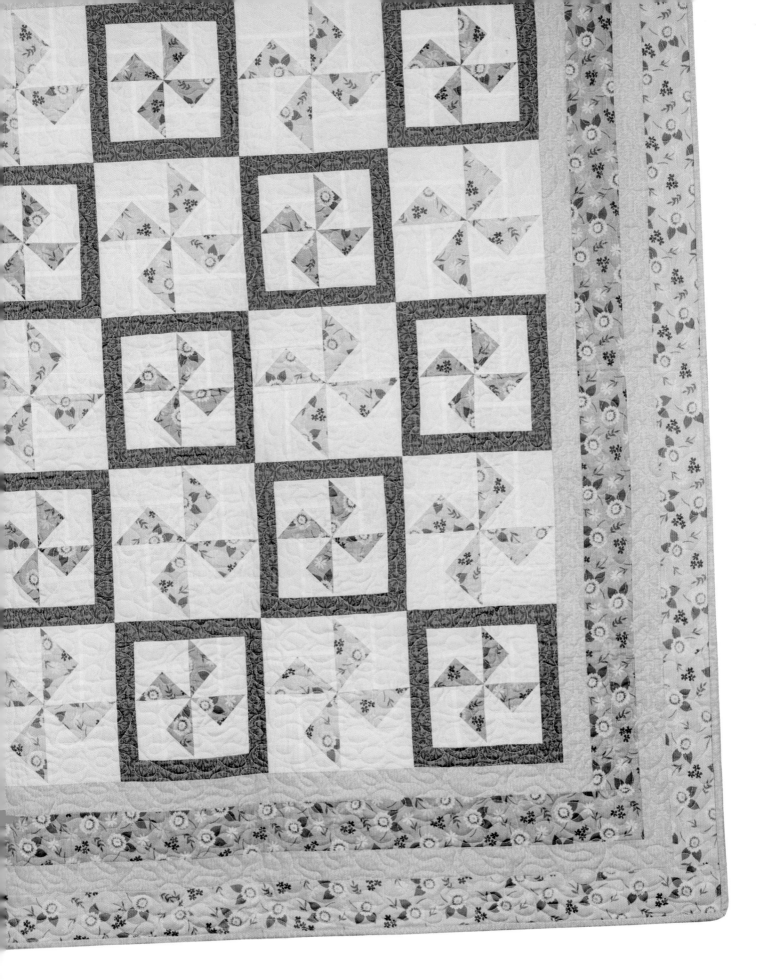

4. Sew a G rectangle to opposite sides and H rectangles to the top and bottom of the block center to complete one Framed Pinwheel block as shown in Figure 6; press.

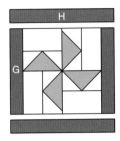

Figure 6

5. Repeat steps 2–4 to complete a total of 10 Framed Pinwheel blocks.

Completing the Quilt

Refer to the Assembly Diagram for positioning of blocks and borders.

1. Arrange and join two each Pinwheel and Framed Pinwheel blocks to make a row; press seams toward the Framed Pinwheel blocks. Repeat to make a total of five rows.

2. Join the rows, turning every other row to create the pattern; press.

3. Join the I/M/N strips on the short ends to make a long strip; press. Subcut strip into two each 2" x 40½" I strips, 2" x 48½" M strips and 2" x 43½" N strips.

4. Sew I strips to opposite long sides and J strips to the top and bottom of the quilt center; press.

5. Join K/L strips on the short ends to make a long strip; press. Subcut strip into two each 3" x 43½" K strips and 3" x 40½" L strips.

6. Sew K strips to opposite long sides and L strips to the top and bottom of the quilt center; press.

7. Sew M strips to opposite long sides and N strips to the top and bottom of the quilt center; press.

8. Repeat step 5 with the O/P strips and subcut into two each 3" x 51½" O strips and 3" x 48½" P strips.

9. Sew O strips to opposite long sides and P strips to the top and bottom of the quilt center to complete the quilt top; press.

10. Layer, quilt and bind referring to Quilting Basics on page 60 to finish. ●

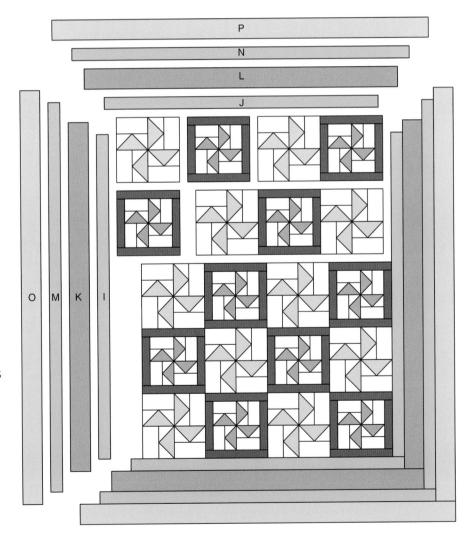

Serenity
Assembly Diagram 48" x 56"

Inspiration

"I really do like the Pinwheel block—any Pinwheel block! In my opinion, it ranks as one of the top blocks for versatility and, as such, is a great inspiration for design. This block also gives the illusion of movement in a quilt. In this case, the block and the fabric inspired me. The quilt seems whisper soft." —Julie Weaver

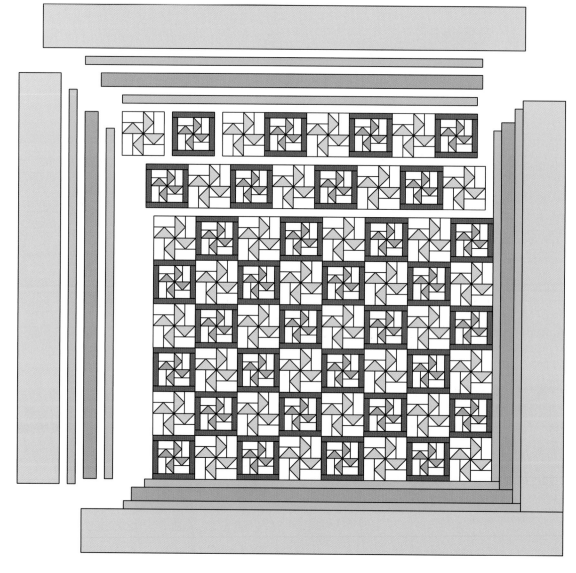

Serenity
Alternate Assembly Diagram 91" x 91"
Add 4 blocks to the width and 3 rows to the length to increase the size of the quilt center.
Increase the size of the outer border strips to 8" finished to make a queen-size quilt.

Three Ways to Make Flying Geese Units

Here are three ways to easily make flying geese units for any of your quilting projects. Try each of these out to find your favorite technique. Then pick a finished size for your project and make a whole flock of flying geese!

Sew & Flip Triangles

With this method, small triangles cut from half-squares are sewn onto opposite sides of a large triangle cut from a quarter-square. The large triangle is the center of the flying geese unit and the small triangles are the "wings."

Cutting

Use a ruler specifically designed for cutting flying geese units, or:

Add 1¼" to the desired finished width of the flying geese unit and cut on both diagonals to make center or large triangles. For example, for a 4" finished width, cut a 5¼" square.

Add ⅞" to the desired finished height of the flying geese unit and cut on one diagonal to make the "wings" or small triangles (Photo A). For example, for a 2" x 4" finished unit, cut 2⅞" squares.

Photo A

Assembly

Place a small triangle, right sides together, on a short side of the larger triangle. Sew a scant ¼" seam.

Open and press to reveal the corner triangle or wing (Photo B).

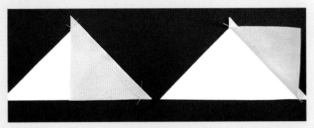

Photo B

Place the second triangle, right sides together, on the opposite short side of the large triangle. The second triangle will slightly overlap the previous triangle. Sew a scant ¼" seam.

Open and press to complete the flying geese unit (Photo C).

Photo C

If desired, trim dog ears and square up the finished unit to the exact size.

Sew, Trim & Flip Rectangles & Squares

With this method, squares are sewn onto opposite ends of a rectangle. The rectangle will be the center of the flying geese unit and the squares will become the "wings." After sewing in place, the squares are trimmed and flipped open to create the unit. The bias edges aren't exposed until after sewing so there is no concern about stretch and distortion.

Cutting

Add ½" to the desired finished height and width of the flying geese unit and cut a rectangle that size.

Cut two squares the same size as the height of the cut rectangle.

For example, to make one 2" x 4" finished flying geese unit, cut a 2½" x 4½" rectangle and two 2½" squares (Photo D).

Photo D

Assembly

Draw a diagonal line from corner to corner on the wrong side of each small square.

Place a square, right sides together, on one end of the rectangle. Sew just inside the drawn line (Photo E).

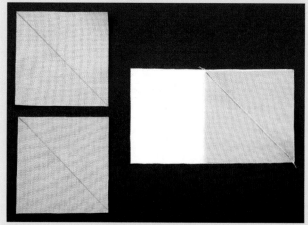

Photo E

Using a rotary cutter, trim ¼" away from sewn line.

Open and press to reveal the corner triangle or wing (Photo F).

Photo F

Place the second square, right sides together, on the opposite end of the rectangle. This square will slightly overlap the previous piece.

Sew just inside the drawn line and trim to ¼" away from sewn line as before.

Open and press to complete the flying geese unit (Photo G).

Photo G

If desired, trim dog ears and square up the finished unit to the exact size.

Four at a Time Alternate

With this method, smaller squares are sewn onto opposite ends of a larger square. The unit is cut in half and additional small squares are sewn on the units. After sewing in place and cutting, the small squares are flipped open to create the flying geese unit.

The large square will be the center of the flying geese units and the small squares will become the "wings." The bias edges aren't exposed until after sewing, so there is no concern about stretch and distortion (Photo H).

Photo H

Cutting

Add 1¼" to the desired finished width of the flying geese unit and cut a square.

Add ⅞" to the height of the desired finished flying geese unit.

For example to make four 2" x 4" finished flying geese units, cut one 5¼" square and 4 (2⅞") squares.

Assembly

Draw a diagonal line on the wrong side of each small square.

Orienting the drawn lines as shown in photo, position two small squares on opposite corners of the large square. The small squares will overlap slightly in the middle.

Stitch ¼" away from both sides of the marked line.

Using a rotary cutter, cut on the marked line to create two units (Photo I).

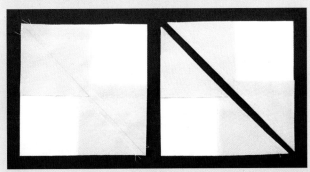

Photo I

Press seam allowances toward the small triangles.

Position the remaining squares on the units as shown and stitch ¼" away from both sides of the marked line (Photo J).

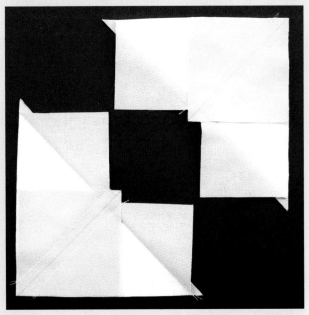

Photo J

Cut on the marked line and press toward the triangles to create a total of four flying geese units (Photo K).

Photo K

If desired, trim dog ears and square up the finished unit to the exact size.

Pinwheels With a Bite

Create stunning pinwheels one block at a time using the paper-piecing method. Challenge yourself to be daring in your color choices and step outside the box.

Designed & Quilted by Deb Karasik

Skill Level

Intermediate

Materials

- ¼ yard multicolored tonal
- ⅜ yard or 1 fat quarter bright-color tonal for each of the 8 Small Bite and 8 Large Bite blocks
- ½ yard teal tonal
- 3⅝ yards black solid
- Backing to size
- Batting to size
- Thread
- Paper
- Basic sewing tools and supplies

Finished Size

Quilt Size: 44" x 44"
Block Sizes: 9" x 9" finished and 3" x 3" finished
Number of Blocks: 16 and 4

Project Notes

Read all instructions before beginning this project. Stitch right sides together using a ¼" seam allowance unless otherwise specified. Refer to a favorite quilting guide for specific techniques. Materials and cutting lists assume 40" of usable fabric width.

Make eight each Large and Small Bite blocks in a variety of colors. For example, your quilt doesn't have to have three blue Small Bite blocks. You might like to make every block a different color. Fat quarters would work perfectly for that type of arrangement.

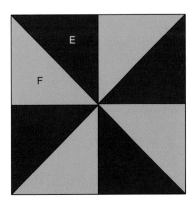

Pinwheel Corner
3" x 3" Finished Block
Make 4

Large Bite
9" x 9" Finished Block
Make 8

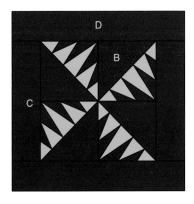

Small Bite
9" x 9" Finished Block
Make 8

Cutting

Prepare paper-piecing patterns for the large and small bite patterns as per patterns found on insert and the Paper Piecing sidebar on page 36.

From multicolored tonal:

- Cut 4 (1½" by fabric width) strips.
   Trim strips to make 2 each 1½" x 36½" G strips and 1½" x 38½" H strips.

From bright-color tonals:

- Cut 20 (2½" x 4½") spike pieces from 1 color for each Large Bite block (a total of 8 blocks).
- Cut 20 (2" x 3½") spike pieces from 1 color for each Small Bite block (a total of 8 blocks).
- Cut 2 (2⅜") squares from each of 4 colors for Pinwheel Corner blocks.
   Cut each square in half on 1 diagonal to make 4 sets of 4 matching F triangles.

From teal tonal:

- Cut 5 (2¼" by fabric width) binding strips.

From black solid:

- Cut 3 (5⅜" by fabric width) strips.
   Subcut strips into 16 (5⅜") squares. Cut each square in half on 1 diagonal to make 32 A triangles.
- Cut 2 (3⅞" by fabric width) strips.
   Subcut strips into 16 (3⅞") squares. Cut each square in half on 1 diagonal to make 32 B triangles.
- Cut 7 (3½" by fabric width) strips.
   Subcut strips into 128 (2" x 3½") small spike pieces for Small Bite blocks. Subcut the remainder of the strips into 8 (2⅜") squares. Cut each square in half on 1 diagonal to make 16 E triangles.
- Cut 8 (4½" by fabric width) strips.
   Subcut strips into 128 (2½" x 4½") large spike pieces for Large Bite blocks.
- Cut 1 (6½" by fabric width) strip.
   Subcut strip into 16 (2" x 6½") C strips.
- Cut 1 (9½" by fabric width) strip.
   Subcut strip into 16 (2" x 9½") D strips.
- Cut 4 (3½" by fabric width) strips.
   Trim strips to make 4 (3½" x 38½") I strips.

Completing the Large Bite Blocks

Refer to the Paper Piecing sidebar on page 36 to make paper-pieced sections.

1. Using the 2½" x 4½" bright-color tonal and black large spike pieces and the Large Bite paper-piecing patterns, complete four large bite sections for each of the eight Large Bite blocks.

2. To complete one Large Bite block, select four matching large bite paper-pieced sections and four A triangles.

3. Sew an A triangle to a large bite section to make a block quarter as shown in Figure 1; press. Repeat to make a total of four block quarters.

Block Quarter
Make 4

Figure 1

4. Join two block quarters to make a row; press. Repeat to make a second row.

5. Join the rows to complete one Large Bite block as shown in Figure 2; press.

Figure 2

6. Repeat steps 2–5 to complete a total of eight Large Bite blocks.

Completing the Small Bite Blocks

1. Repeat steps 1–5 for Completing the Large Bite Blocks, except use the Small Bite paper-piecing patterns with 2" x 3½" bright-color tonal and black small spike pieces and add B triangles to complete the block center as shown in Figure 3.

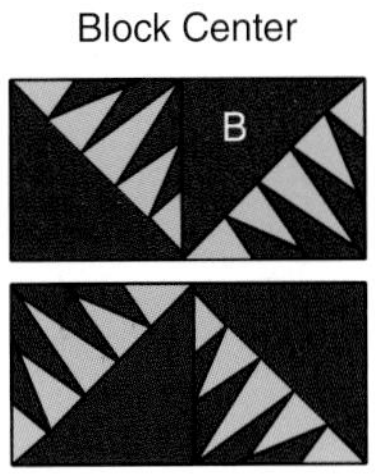

Block Center

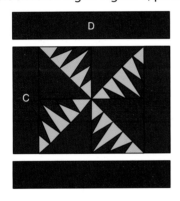

Figure 3

2. Sew a C strip to opposite sides and D strips to the top and bottom of the block center to complete one Small Bite block referring to Figure 4; press.

Figure 4

3. Repeat steps 1 and 2 to complete a total of eight Small Bite blocks.

Completing the Pinwheel Corner Blocks

1. Select four matching F and four E triangles for one block. ***Note:*** *If you prefer, you may paper-piece these blocks using the Pinwheel Corner Paper-Piecing Pattern found on insert. See Here's a Tip.*

Here's a Tip

A paper-piecing pattern has been given for the Pinwheel Corner block sections. You may make these blocks without using the paper-piecing patterns, but if matching seams on small pieces scares you, you can make perfect blocks using the paper-piecing patterns.

2. Sew an E triangle to an F triangle to make an E-F unit as shown in Figure 5; press. Repeat to make a total of four E-F units.

E-F Unit
Make 4

Figure 5

3. Join two E-F units to make a row; press. Repeat to make a second row.

4. Join the two rows to complete one Pinwheel Corner block as shown in Figure 6; press.

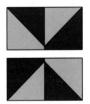

Figure 6

5. Repeat steps 1–4 to complete a total of four different-color Pinwheel Corner blocks.

Completing the Quilt

Refer to the Assembly Diagram for positioning of blocks and borders.

1. Arrange and join two each Large and Small Bite blocks to make four rows; press. Join the rows to complete the quilt center; press.

2. Sew G strips to opposite sides and H strips to the top and bottom of the quilt center; press.

3. Remove all paper patterns from paper-pieced sections in completed quilt center.

4. Sew an I strip to opposite sides of the quilt center; press.

5. Sew a Pinwheel Corner block to each end of each remaining I strip; press. Sew these strips to the top and bottom of the quilt center to complete the quilt top; press. Remove paper patterns from blocks if paper-pieced.

6. Layer, quilt and bind referring to Quilting Basics on page 60 to finish. ●

Inspiration

"I was inspired by the Pinwheel pattern but felt it needed just a little more 'bite.'" —Deb Karasik

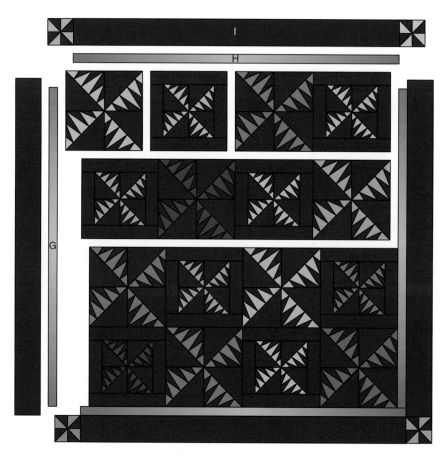

Pinwheels With a Bite
Assembly Diagram 44" x 44"

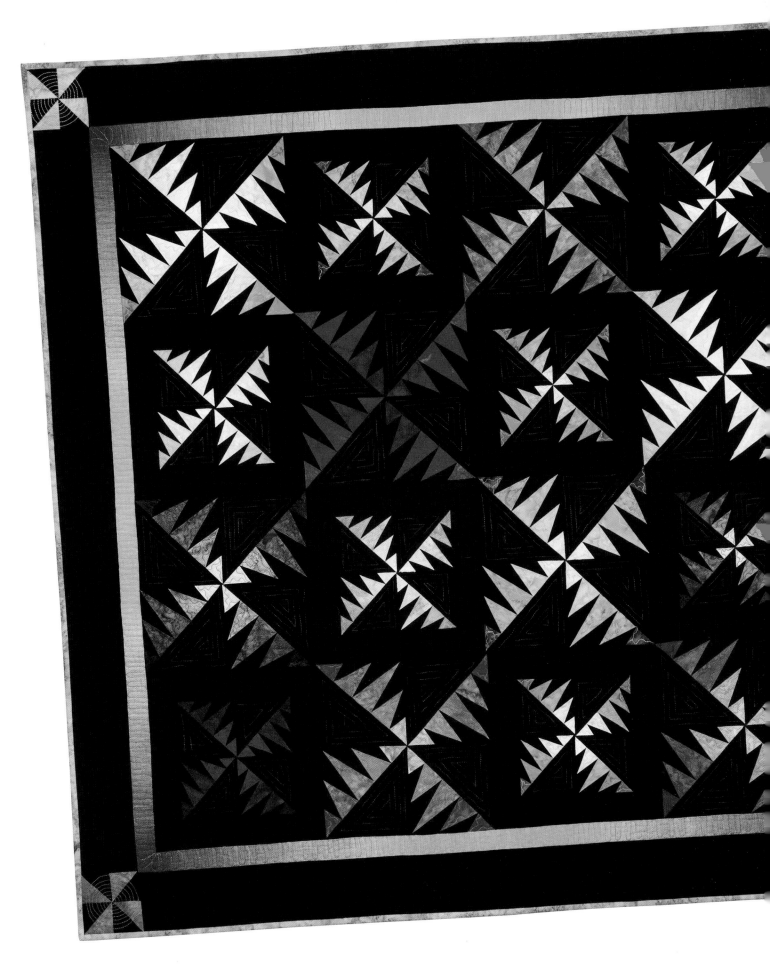

Paper Piecing

One of the oldest quilting techniques, paper piecing allows a quilter to make blocks with odd-shaped and/or small pieces. The paper is carefully removed when the block is completed. The following instructions are for one type of paper-piecing technique; refer to a comprehensive quilting guide for other types of paper piecing.

1. Make same-size photocopies of the paper-piecing pattern given as directed on the pattern. There are several choices in regular papers as well as water-soluble papers that can be used, which are available at your local office-supply store, quilt shop or online.

2. Cut out the patterns leaving a margin around the outside bold lines as shown in Figure A. All patterns are reversed on the paper copies. Pattern color choices can be written in each numbered space on the marked side of each copy.

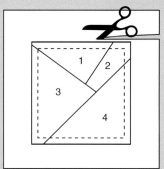

Figure A

3. When cutting fabric for paper piecing, the pieces do not have to be the exact size and shape of the area to be covered. Cut fabric pieces the general shape and ¼"–½" larger than the design area to be covered. This makes paper-piecing a good way to use up scraps.

4. With the printed side of the pattern facing you, fold along each line of the pattern as shown in Figure B, creasing the stitching lines. This will help in trimming the fabric seam allowances and in removing the paper when you are finished stitching.

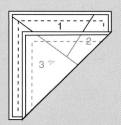

Figure B

5. Turn the paper pattern over with the unmarked side facing you and position fabric indicated on pattern right side up over the space marked 1. Hold the paper up to a window or over a light box to make sure that the fabric overlaps all sides of space 1 at least ¼" from the printed side of the pattern as shown in Figure C. Pin to hold fabric in place. **Note:** You can also use a light touch of glue stick. Too much glue will make the paper difficult to remove.

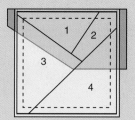

Figure C

6. Turn the paper over with the right side of the paper facing you, and fold the paper along the lines between sections 1 and 2. Trim fabric to about ¼" from the folded edge as shown in Figure D.

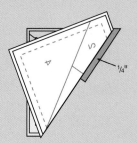

Figure D

7. *Place the second fabric indicated right sides together with first piece. Fabric edges should be even along line between spaces 1 and 2 as shown in Figure E. Fold fabric over and check to see if second fabric piece will cover space 2.*

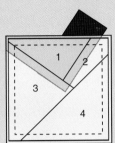

Figure E

8. *With the right side of the paper facing you, hold fabric pieces together and stitch along the line between spaces 1 and 2 as shown in Figure F using a very small stitch length (18–20 stitches per inch).* **Note:** *Using a smaller stitch length will make removing paper easier because it creates a tear line at the seam. Always begin and end seam by sewing two to three stitches beyond the line. You do not need to backstitch. When the beginning of the seam is at the edge of the pattern, start sewing at the solid outside line of the pattern.*

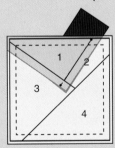

Figure F

9. *Turn the pattern over, flip the second fabric back and finger-press as shown in Figure G.*

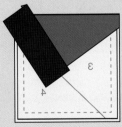

Figure G

10. *Continue trimming and sewing pieces in numerical order until the pattern is completely covered. Make sure pieces along the outer edge extend past the solid line to allow for a ¼" seam allowance as shown in Figure H.*

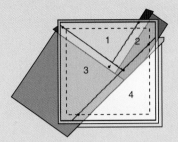

Figure H

11. *When the entire block is sewn, press the block and trim all excess fabric from the block along the outside-edge solid line of paper pattern as shown in Figure I.*

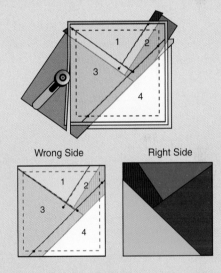

Wrong Side   Right Side

Figure I

12. *After stitching blocks together, carefully remove the backing paper from completed blocks and press seams. Or, staystitch ⅛" from the outer edge of the completed block. Carefully remove backing paper and press seams. Then complete quilt top assembly.*

A Quilter's Wreath

Easy piecing and a bit of appliqué are the skills
you need to create a holiday moment.

Design by Gina Gempesaw
Machine-Quilted by Carole Whaling

Skill Level
Confident Beginner

Finished Size
Quilt Size: 39" x 39"
Block Size: 6" x 6" finished
Number of Blocks: 16

Materials
- 26 assorted red scraps at least 4" square
- 1 fat eighth light green tonal
- ¼ yard gold tonal
- ⅝ yard dark green tonal
- 1⅔ yards white solid
- Backing to size
- Batting to size
- Thread
- Tracing paper
- 1 yard fusible web
- Basic sewing tools and supplies

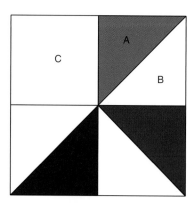

Partial Pinwheel
6" x 6" Finished Block
Make 12

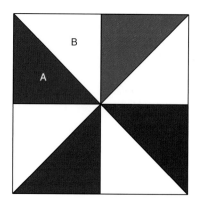

Pinwheel
6" x 6" Finished Block
Make 4

Project Notes
Read all instructions before beginning this project.
Stitch right sides together using a ¼" seam allowance
unless otherwise specified. Refer to a favorite quilting
guide for specific techniques. Materials and cutting
lists assume 40" of usable fabric width.

Cutting
Prepare templates for ribbon using pattern given in
the insert. Prepare for appliqué as per pattern in the
insert and referring to Raw-Edge Fusible Appliqué
on page 42.

From assorted red scraps:
- Cut 26 (3⅞") squares.
    Cut each square in half on 1 diagonal to make
    52 A triangles.

From light green tonal:
- Cut 2 (3½" x 20") D strips.

From dark green tonal:
- Cut 1 (1½" by fabric width) strip.
  Subcut strip into 12 (1½") F squares.
- Cut 5 (2¼" by fabric width) binding strips.

From white solid:
- Cut 3 (3⅞" by fabric width) strips.
  Subcut strips into 26 (3⅞") squares. Cut each square in half on 1 diagonal to make 52 B triangles.
- Cut 2 (3½" by fabric width) strips.
  Subcut strips into 12 (3½") C squares.
- Cut 2 (2" by fabric width) strips.
  Cut each strip in half to make 4 (2" x 20") E strips.
- Cut 1 (6½" by fabric width) strip.
  Subcut strip into 4 (1½" x 6½") G strips and 4 (6½" x 7½") H rectangles.
- Cut 1 (8½" by fabric width) strip.
  Subcut strip into 2 (6½" x 8½") I rectangles and 1 (8½" x 20½") J rectangle.
- Cut 4 (3" by fabric width) strips.
  Trim strips to make 2 each 3" x 34½" K strips and 3" x 39½" L strips.

Completing the Blocks

1. Sew an A triangle to a B triangle to make an A-B unit as shown in Figure 1; press seam toward B. Repeat to make a total of 52 A-B units.

A-B Unit
Make 52

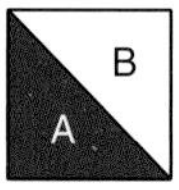

Figure 1

2. Select four A-B units. Join two units to make a row; press. Repeat to make a second row. Join the rows to complete one Pinwheel block as shown in Figure 2. Repeat to make a total of four Pinwheel blocks.

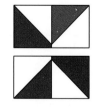

Figure 2

3. Select three A-B units and a C square to make a Partial Pinwheel block.

4. Sew the C square to an A-B unit to make a row; press. Join two A-B units to make a row; press. Join the rows to complete one Partial Pinwheel block as shown in Figure 3; press.

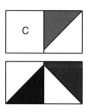

Figure 3

5. Repeat steps 3 and 4 to complete a total of 12 Partial Pinwheel blocks.

Completing the Quilt Top
Refer to the Assembly Diagram for positioning of blocks, sashing strips, rectangles and borders.

1. Sew an E strip to opposite long sides of a D strip to make a D-E strip set; press. Repeat to make a second D-E strip set.

2. Subcut D-E strip sets into 20 (1½" x 6½") D-E units as shown in Figure 4.

D-E Unit
Cut 20
1½"

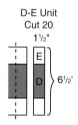

6½'

Figure 4

3. Join three D-E units with four F squares and two G strips to make a sashing row as shown in Figure 5; press. Repeat to make a second sashing row.

Sashing Row
Make 2

Figure 5

4. Join one Pinwheel block and two Partial Pinwheel blocks with two D-E units, and add an H rectangle to each end; press. Sew a sashing row to the bottom to make the top row; press. Repeat to make the bottom row.

5. Join four Partial Pinwheel blocks with two D-E units and one I rectangle to make row 2; press. Repeat to make row 4.

6. Sew an F square to each end of two D-E units to make a D-E-F unit as shown in Figure 6; press. Repeat to make a second D-E-F unit.

D-E-F Unit
Make 2

Figure 6

7. Sew a D-E-F unit to opposite ends of J to make the center unit; press.

8. Sew a D-E unit to the top and bottom of each remaining Pinwheel block and sew these units to each end of the center unit to complete the center row; press.

9. Join the rows to complete the quilt center; press.

10. Sew K strips to the top and bottom and L strips to opposite sides of the quilt center to complete the quilt top piecing; press.

11. Prepare each bow piece for appliqué referring to pattern in insert and Raw-Edge Fusible Appliqué on page 42.

12. Arrange, fuse and stitch the appliqué pieces to the pieced quilt top in numerical order referring to the pattern and Figure 7.

13. Layer, quilt and bind referring to Quilting Basics on page 60 to finish. ●

Figure 7

Inspiration

*"I wanted to create a fast wreath quilt.
The Pinwheel block is perfect for this project."*
—Gina Gempesaw

Here's a Tip

Use a purchased 1½"-wide ribbon to replace the appliquéd bow if desired. Tie the ribbon into a large bow and hand-tack it in place on the quilted and bound wall quilt.

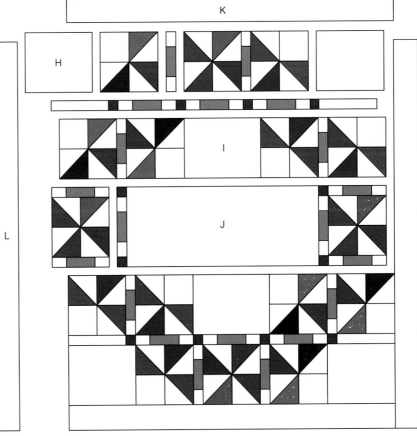

A Quilter's Wreath
Assembly Diagram 39" x 39"

Raw-Edge Fusible Appliqué

One of the easiest ways to appliqué is the fusible-web method. Paper-backed fusible web motifs are fused to the wrong side of fabric, cut out and then fused to a foundation fabric and stitched in place by hand or machine. You can use this method for raw- or turned-edge appliqué.

1. If the appliqué motif is directional, it should be reversed for raw-edge fusible appliqué. If doing several identical appliqué motifs, trace reversed motif shapes onto template material to make reusable templates.

2. Use templates or trace the appliqué motif shapes onto paper side of paper-backed fusible web. Leave at least ½" between shapes. Cut out shapes leaving a margin around traced lines.

3. Follow manufacturer's instructions and fuse shapes to wrong side of fabric as indicated on pattern for color and number to cut.

4. Cut out appliqué shapes on traced lines and remove paper backing from fusible web.

5. Again following manufacturer's instructions, arrange and fuse pieces on the foundation fabric referring to appliqué motif included in pattern.

6. Hand- or machine-stitch around edges. *Note: Position a light- to medium-weight stabilizer behind the appliqué motif to keep the fabric from puckering during machine stitching. Some stitch possibilities are satin or zigzag, buttonhole, blanket or running stitch.*

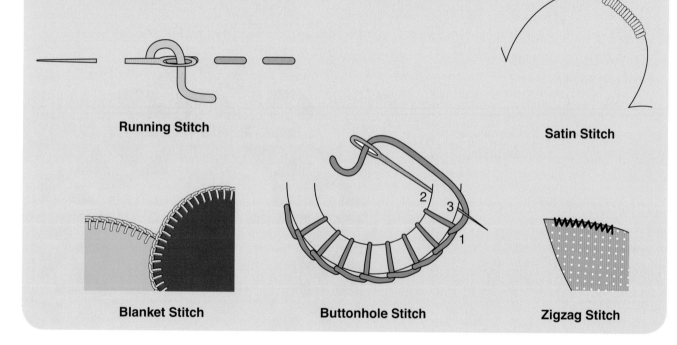

Running Stitch

Satin Stitch

Blanket Stitch

Buttonhole Stitch

Zigzag Stitch

Flutter Pinwheels

Make graceful pinwheels and create movement with the help of templates. The subtle curves are easy to piece yet add a touch of elegance to this quilt top.

Designed & Quilted by Holly Daniels

Skill Level
Intermediate

Finished Size
Quilt Size: 60" x 60"
Block Size: 12" x 12" finished
Number of Blocks: 16

Materials
- 2⅞ yards light peach tonal
- 3 yards dark peach floral
- Backing to size
- Batting to size
- Thread
- Template material
- Basic sewing tools and supplies

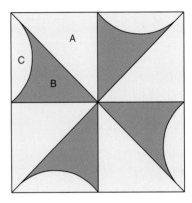

Flutter Pinwheel
12" x 12" Finished Block
Make 16

Project Notes

Read all instructions before beginning this project. Stitch right sides together using a ¼" seam allowance unless otherwise specified. Refer to a favorite quilting guide for specific techniques. Materials and cutting lists assume 40" of usable fabric width.

Cutting

Prepare templates for B and C pieces using patterns given on insert. Refer to patterns and Completing the Blocks for cutting.

From light peach tonal:

- Cut 7 (6⅞" by fabric width) strips.
   Subcut strips into 32 (6⅞") squares. Cut each square in half on 1 diagonal to make 64 A triangles.
- Cut 4 (6½" by fabric width) C strips.
   Cut C pieces from the strips as per template and step 2 of Completing the Blocks.
- Cut 6 (2½" by fabric width) D/E strips.

From dark peach floral:

- Cut 7 (6⅞" by fabric width) strips.
   Subcut strips into 32 (6⅞") squares. Cut each square in half on 1 diagonal to make 64 triangles. Use B template to cut B pieces as per step 1 of Completing the Blocks.
- Cut 6 (4½" by fabric width) F/G strips.
- Cut 7 (2¼" by fabric width) binding strips.

Completing the Blocks

1. Trace the B template on the wrong side of the B triangles as shown in Figure 1; cut out on marked lines. Transfer the matching marks from the template to each piece.

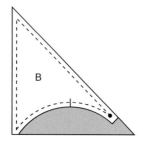

Figure 1

2. Trace template C on the wrong side of the C strips as shown in Figure 2. Repeat to trace a total of 64 C pieces; cut out on marked lines. Transfer the matching marks from the template to each piece.

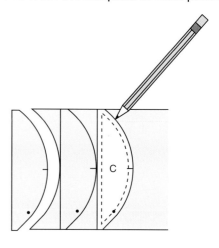

Figure 2

Here's a Tip

Use sandpaper dots on the back of plastic templates when tracing onto fabric to prevent slipping.

3. Matching the marks, sew a C piece to a B piece to complete a B-C unit referring to Figure 3 and Curved Piecing on page 12; press. Repeat to make a total of 64 B-C units.

Figure 3

4. To complete one Flutter Pinwheel block, select four each A triangles and B-C units.

5. Sew a B-C unit to A to make an A-B-C unit as shown in Figure 4; press. Repeat to make a total of four A-B-C units.

A-B-C Unit
Make 4

Figure 4

6. Join two A-B-C units to make a row; press. Repeat to make a second row. Join the rows to complete one Flutter Pinwheel block as shown in Figure 5; press.

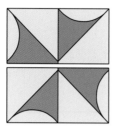

Figure 5

7. Repeat steps 4–6 to complete a total of 16 Flutter Pinwheel blocks.

Completing the Quilt Top

Refer to the Assembly Diagram for positioning of blocks and borders.

1. Join four Flutter Pinwheel blocks to make a row; press. Repeat to make a total of four rows.

2. Join the rows to complete the quilt center; press.

3. Join the D/E strips on the short ends to make a long strip; press. Subcut strip into two each 2½" x 48½" D strips and 2½" x 52½" E strips.

4. Sew D strips to opposite sides and E strips to the top and bottom of the quilt center; press.

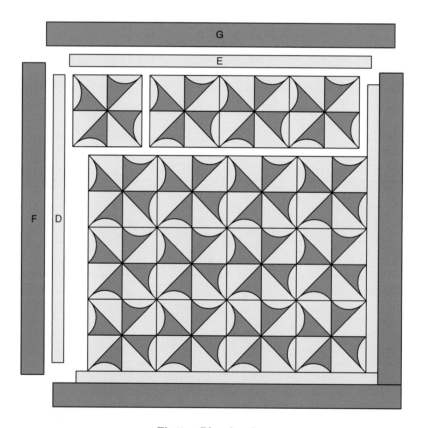

Flutter Pinwheels
Assembly Diagram 60" x 60"

5. Join the F/G strips on the short ends to make a long strip; press. Subcut strip into two each 4½" x 52½" F strips and 4½" x 60½" G strips.

6. Sew F strips to opposite sides and G strips to the top and bottom of the quilt center to complete the quilt top; press.

7. Layer, quilt and bind referring to Quilting Basics on page 60 to finish. ●

Inspiration

"I was actually thinking about fluttery butterfly wings when I designed this quilt. I make many scrap quilts, but I liked the calming effect of using only two colors this time." —Holly Daniels

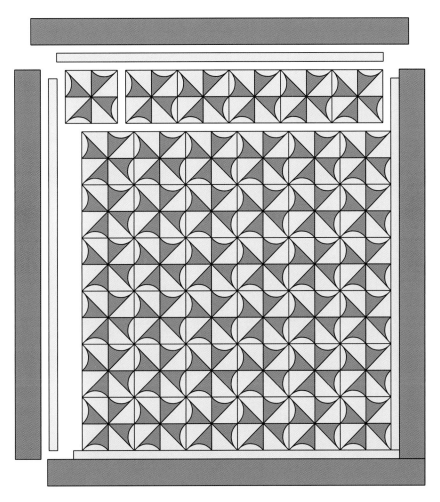

Flutter Pinwheels
Alternate Assembly Diagram 88" x 100"
Add 2 blocks to the width and 3 rows to the length to increase the size of the quilt center. Increase the size of the outer border strips to 6" finished to make a queen-size quilt.

Pinwheel Garden

If you're ready for a challenge, this is the quilt for you.
Block placement creates the garden path with accents
of broderie perse appliqué as the garden.

Designed & Quilted by Jo Moury

Skill Level
Intermediate

Finished Size
Quilt Size: 59½" x 59½"
Block Size: 8" x 8" finished
Number of Blocks: 25

Materials
- ⅛ yard medium blue solid
- ⅛ yard lavender solid
- ¼ yard yellow solid
- ¼ yard light blue solid
- ½ yard medium green solid
- ½ yard orange solid
- ½ yard large floral
- 1⅛ yards purple tonal
- 2 yards coordinating floral border stripe
- 3⅛ yards white solid
- Backing to size
- Batting to size
- Thread
- Template material
- Basic sewing tools and supplies

Project Notes
Read all instructions before beginning this project.
Stitch right sides together using a ¼" seam allowance
unless otherwise specified. Refer to a favorite quilting
guide for specific techniques. Materials and cutting
lists assume 40" of usable fabric width.

Cutting
Prepare templates for F, P, M, N, and T pieces and
Right and Left Ribbon Ends using patterns given
on insert; cut as directed on each piece. Cut large
floral motifs for appliqué referring to Broderie Perse
Appliqué on page 58.

From medium blue solid:
- Cut 1 (2¾" by fabric width) strip.
    Subcut strip into 10 (2¾") squares. Cut each
        square in half on 1 diagonal to make
        20 L triangles.

From lavender solid:
- Cut F and FR pieces as per pattern.

From yellow solid:
- Cut 2 (2⅛" by fabric width) strips.
    Subcut strips into 26 (2⅛") squares.
        Cut each square in half on 1 diagonal to
        make 52 O triangles.

From light blue solid:
- Cut 1 (2⅛" by fabric width) strip.
    Subcut strip into 16 (2⅛") squares. Cut each
        square in half on 1 diagonal to make
        32 S triangles.
- Cut 1 (2⅞" by fabric width) strip.
    Subcut strip into 8 (2⅞") squares. Cut each square
        in half on 1 diagonal to make 16 G triangles.

From medium green solid:
- Cut 1 (5½" by fabric width) strip.
    Subcut strip into 4 each 1½" x 5½" CC and
        1½" x 4½" BB rectangles and 8 each 1½" x 1¾"
        GG and 1½" x 3¼" V rectangles.

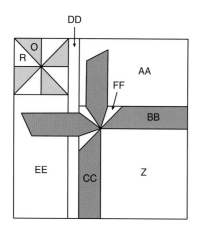

Corner Pinwheel
8" x 8" Finished Block
Make 4

Here's a Tip

Because there are so many pieces in the Pinwheel Garden quilt, and some are so close in size, it is helpful to pin all same-letter pieces together with a note stating the letter of the piece. When instructed to use particular pieces while piecing units or blocks, you will be able to find each piece easily.

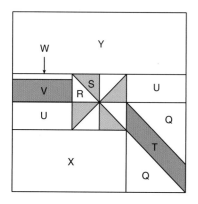

Side Pinwheel
8" x 8" Finished Block
Make 4

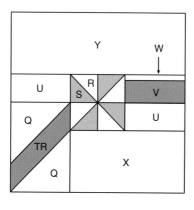

Reverse Side Pinwheel
8" x 8" Finished Block
Make 4

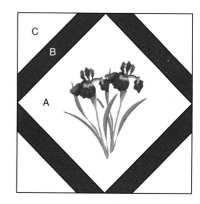

Flower
8" x 8" Finished Block
Make 4

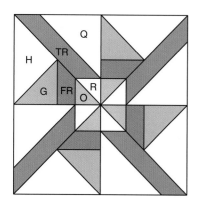

Reverse Spinning Pinwheel
8" x 8" Finished Block
Make 2

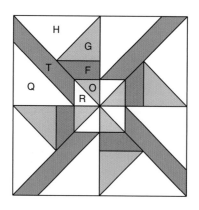

Spinning Pinwheel
8" x 8" Finished Block
Make 2

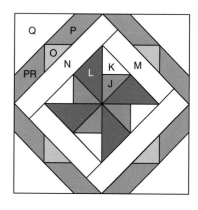

Framed Pinwheel
8" x 8" Finished Block
Make 5

- Cut 1 (2⅛" by fabric width) strip.
    Subcut strip into 6 (2⅛") squares. Cut each square in half on 1 diagonal to make 12 JJ triangles.
- Cut T and TR pieces and ribbon ends as per pattern.

From orange solid:
- Cut 2 (2⅛" by fabric width) strips.
    Subcut strips into 20 (2⅛") squares. Cut each square in half on 1 diagonal to make 40 HH triangles.
- Cut 1 (3⅛" by fabric width) strip.
    Subcut strip into 5 (3⅛") squares. Cut each square on both diagonals to make 20 J triangles.
- Cut P and PR pieces as per pattern.

From large floral:
- Cut four floral motifs to fit the A squares for appliqué referring to Broderie Perse Appliqué on page 58.

From purple tonal:
- Cut 2 (4½" by fabric width) strips.
    Subcut strips into 16 (4½") B squares.
- Cut 1 (2⅛" by fabric width) strip.
    Subcut strip into 16 (2⅛") squares. Cut each square in half on 1 diagonal to make 32 II triangles.
- Cut 7 (2¼" by fabric width) binding strips.

From coordinating floral border stripe:
- Cut 4 (5½" x 66") I strips along length of stripe.

From white solid:
- Cut 2 (8½" by fabric width) strips.
    Subcut strips into 4 (8½") A squares, 16 (1¾" x 8½") D strips and 4 (1" x 8½") DD strips.
- Cut 9 (3¼" by fabric width) strips.
    Subcut strips into 88 (1¾" x 3¼") U rectangles, 16 (3¼") C squares, and 8 each ¾" x 3¼" W, 3¼" x 5¾" X and 3¼" x 8½" Y rectangles.
- Cut 3 (3⅝" by fabric width) strips.
    Subcut strips into 26 (3⅝") Q squares, 8 (1¾" x 3½") KK strips and 4 (2½") FF squares. Cut each Q square in half on 1 diagonal to make 52 Q triangles.

- Cut 5 (2⅛" by fabric width) strips.
    Subcut strips into 74 (2⅛") squares. Cut each square in half on 1 diagonal to make 148 R triangles.
- Cut 1 (4½" by fabric width) strip.
    Subcut strip into 8 (1¾" x 4½") LL strips and 4 (4½") Z squares.
- Cut 1 (6" by fabric width) strip.
    Subcut strip into 4 each 3½" x 5½" AA rectangles and 3" x 6" EE rectangles and 24 (1¾") E squares.
- Cut 1 (5¼" by fabric width) strip.
    Subcut strip into 4 (5¼") H squares and 5 (3⅛") K squares. Cut each square on both diagonals to make 16 H triangles and 20 K triangles.
- Cut 5 (1½" by fabric width) MM/NN strips.
- Cut M and N pieces as per patterns.

Completing the Flower Blocks

1. Draw a diagonal line from corner to corner on the wrong side of each B and C square.

2. Referring to Figure 1, place a B square right sides together on opposite corners of an A square and stitch on the marked lines. Trim seam allowances to ¼" and press B to the right side.

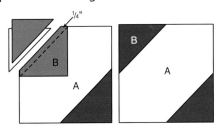

Figure 1

3. Repeat step 2 on the remaining corners of A to complete an A-B unit as shown in Figure 2.

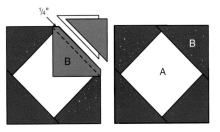

Figure 2

4. Repeat steps 2 and 3 with C squares to complete the block background as shown in Figure 3.

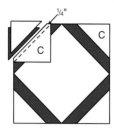

Figure 3

5. To complete one Flower block, prepare floral motifs and arrange on the A center of the block background and stitch in place referring to Figure 4 and Broderie Perse Appliqué on page 58.

Figure 4

6. Repeat steps 2–5 to complete a total of four Flower blocks.

Completing the Framed Pinwheel Blocks

1. Sew a J triangle to a K triangle and add L to make a J-K-L unit as shown in Figure 5; press. Repeat to make a total of four J-K-L units.

J-K-L Unit
Make 4

Figure 5

2. Join two J-K-L units to make a row; press. Repeat to make a second row. Join the rows to complete the block center as shown in Figure 6.

Figure 6

3. Sew M to opposite sides and N to the top and bottom of the block center as shown in Figure 7; press.

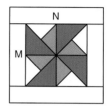

Figure 7

4. Sew P and PR to opposite short sides of O and add Q to make a corner unit as shown in Figure 8; press. Repeat to make a total of four corner units.

Corner Unit
Make 4

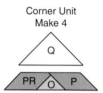

Figure 8

5. Sew a corner unit to each side of the framed block center to complete one Framed Pinwheel block as shown in Figure 9; press.

Figure 9

6. Repeat steps 1–5 to complete a total of five Framed Pinwheel blocks.

Completing the Spinning Pinwheel Blocks

1. Sew R to T and add Q to make a Q-R-T unit as shown in Figure 10; press.

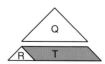

Figure 10

2. Sew O to F; press. Sew G to H; press. Join the two units to make an F-G-H-O unit as shown in Figure 11; press.

Figure 11

3. Sew the Q-R-T unit to the F-G-H-O unit to complete a block quarter as shown in Figure 12; press.

Block Quarter
Make 4

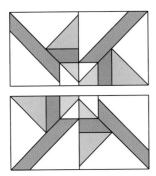

Figure 12

4. Repeat steps 1–3 to complete a total of four block quarters.

5. Join two block quarters to make a row; press. Repeat to make a second row. Join the rows as shown in Figure 13 to complete one Spinning Pinwheel block; press.

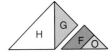

Figure 13

6. Repeat steps 1–5 to complete a total of two Spinning Pinwheel blocks.

7. Repeat steps 1–5, using FR and TR pieces to make reverse units as shown in Figure 14, to complete two Reverse Spinning Pinwheel blocks as shown in Figure 15.

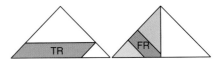

Figure 14

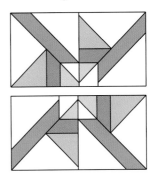

Figure 15

Completing the Side Pinwheel Blocks

1. Sew R to S to make an R-S unit as shown in Figure 16; press. Repeat to make a total of four R-S units.

R-S Unit
Make 4

Figure 16

2. Join two R-S units to make a row; press. Repeat to make a second row. Join the rows to complete a pinwheel unit as shown in Figure 17; press.

Figure 17

3. Sew W to V to U and sew to the pinwheel unit as shown in Figure 18; press.

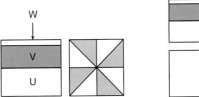

Figure 18   **Figure 19**

4. Add X to the pieced unit to complete the corner unit as shown in Figure 19; press.

5. Sew Q to opposite sides of T and add U to make a Q-T-U unit as shown in Figure 20; press.

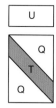

Figure 20

6. Sew the Q-T-U unit to the corner unit and add Y to make a Side Pinwheel block as shown in Figure 21; press.

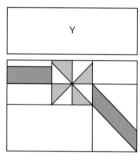

Figure 21

7. Repeat steps 1–6 to make a total of four Side Pinwheel blocks.

8. Repeat steps 1-6 using TR pieces as shown in Figure 22 to make four Reverse Side Pinwheel blocks.

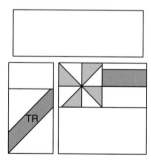

Figure 22

Completing the Corner Pinwheel Blocks

1. Draw a diagonal line from corner to corner on the wrong side of each FF square.

2. Sew BB to Z and add CC to make a Z-BB-CC unit as shown in Figure 23; press.

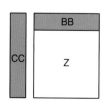

Figure 23

3. Referring to Figure 24, place the FF square right sides together on the pieced corner of the Z-BB-CC unit and stitch on the marked line; trim seam allowance to ¼" and press FF to the right side to complete the corner unit.

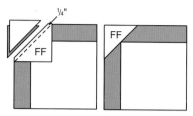

Figure 24

4. Sew AA to the BB side and DD to the CC side of the corner unit to make a half unit as shown in Figure 25; press.

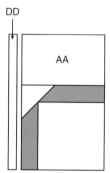

Figure 25

5. Sew O to R to make an O-R unit as shown in Figure 26; press. Repeat to make a total of four O-R units.

O-R Unit
Make 4

Figure 26

6. Join two O-R units to make a row; press. Repeat to make a second row. Join the rows to complete the pinwheel unit as shown in Figure 27; press.

Figure 27

7. Sew EE to the pinwheel unit; press. Sew this unit to the previously pieced half unit to complete the base for one Corner Pinwheel block as shown in Figure 28; press.

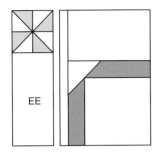

Figure 28

8. Turn under seam allowance of a right ribbon end and a left ribbon end piece and hand-appliqué pieces in place at the corner of BB and CC to complete one Corner Pinwheel block as shown in Figure 29.

Figure 29

9. Repeat steps 1–8 to complete a total of four Corner Pinwheel blocks.

Completing the Sashing Units

1. Sew II to R to make an II-R unit as shown in Figure 30; press. Repeat to make a total of 32 II-R units.

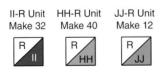

Figure 30

2. Repeat step 1 with HH and R to make a total of 40 HH-R units and with JJ and R to make a total of 12 JJ-R units, again referring to Figure 30.

3. Join two II-R units to make a purple unit as shown in Figure 31; press. Repeat to make a total of 16 purple units.

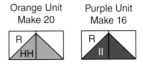

Figure 31

4. Repeat step 3 with HH-R units to make 20 orange units, again referring to Figure 31.

5. Sew a U rectangle to the ends of each purple and orange unit to make 16 purple and 20 orange sashing strips as shown in Figure 32; press.

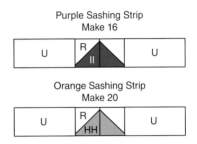

Figure 32

6. Sew KK to one 1¾" edge of GG and LL to the opposite edge to complete a green sashing strip as shown in Figure 33; press. Repeat to make a total of eight green sashing strips.

Figure 33

Completing the Quilt

Refer to the Assembly Diagram for arrangement of blocks and sashing strips for block rows and positioning of sashing units and strips for sashing rows.

1. Arrange and join the blocks in five rows of five blocks each inserting orange, purple or green sashing or D strips in rows as needed; press.

2. Join E squares, JJ-R units and D strips with green, orange or purple sashing strips to make six sashing rows; press.

3. Join the block rows with the sashing rows to complete the quilt center; press.

4. Join the MM/NN strips on the short ends to make a long strip; press. Subcut strip into two each 1½" x 48" MM strips and 1½" x 50" NN strips.

5. Sew the MM strips to opposite sides and NN strips to the top and bottom of the quilt center; press.

6. Center and sew an I strip to opposite sides and to the top and bottom of the quilt center, stopping stitching ¼" from corners of the quilt center.

7. Miter corners, trim seams to ¼" and press corner seams open to complete the quilt top.

8. Layer, quilt and bind referring to Quilting Basics on page 60 to finish. ●

Inspiration

"Sometimes a design leads to fabric selection, and sometimes, it is the other way around. I saw Botanical Blues on the Northcott website and fell in love with the realistic flowers. I really like to combine blocks so that the lines blend together and flow from one block to another. When the call came for a pinwheel submission, I didn't hesitate to play with the Botanical Blue collection. I truly like how the pinwheels all play together suggesting different flowers in a formal English garden while the green fabric paints the pathways across the quilt." —Jo Moury

COLOR KEY
- Medium blue solid
- Lavender solid
- Yellow solid
- Light blue solid
- Medium green solid
- Orange solid
- Large floral
- Purple tonal
- Floral border stripe
- White solid

Pinwheel Garden
Assembly Diagram 59¹⁄₂" x 59¹⁄₂"

Broderie Perse Appliqué

In the early 1700s, a chintz printed fabric from India began to become popular in England. The original prints were based on fashionable Indian themes that had clearly defined motifs with separations between them.

Later oriental themes were added making the fabric an odd mix of East and West. Most popular was the Tree of Life design that included a large tree with a wide variety of birds and flowers.

An import ban on the fabric, influenced by the English textile industry, made it difficult to find and expensive. However, it remained a popular fabric because quilters used an ingenious technique of cutting out motifs from the original design and appliquéing them to a background fabric. Using this technique meant that quilters did not need as much of the chintz to make a whole quilt.

The French term "broderie perse" translates as Persian embroidery and has been used for this appliqué technique from the beginning, despite the fact that the fabrics were not Persian. It is also referred to as chintz embroidery.

It became increasingly popular to make medallion quilts using broderie perse in the late 1700s to mid-1800s. By matching the background to the background color of the chintz, the motif did not need to be trimmed as close, and a simple straight stitch could be used to stitch the pieces together.

You can skip a lot of the preparatory steps for traditional appliqué when using the broderie perse technique. Since you are using the printed motifs, there are no templates and no tracing to deal with.

Choose fabrics with similar colors and motifs of similar size and scale with space enough between them to isolate individual motifs.

Cut out individual motifs. Play with the arrangement until you are happy with the composition.

To make a broderie perse block or quilt:

1. Select a variety of motifs from a printed fabric that has a large open design.

2. Cut pieces of double-sided, self-stick fusible web and fuse to the back of the selected motif areas.

3. Cut out the motifs following the edges of the motifs, or leave a ⅛" margin of background color around each motif. Prepare as many motifs as desired.

4. Position the motifs on the blocks or quilt arranging and rearranging for the desired look.

5. Fuse the motifs in place following the manufacturer's instructions when satisfied with the arrangement.

6. Motifs should be stitched in place to secure. Use a machine straight stitch close to cut edges or turn cut edges to wrong side slightly and stitch using a small machine blanket or buttonhole stitch. Use thread the same color as the background of the printed fabric.

Quilting Basics
The following is a reference guide. For more information, consult a comprehensive quilting book.

Always:
- Read through the entire pattern before you begin your project.
- Purchase quality, 100 percent cotton fabrics.
- When considering prewashing, do so with ALL of the fabrics being used. Generally, prewashing is not required in quilting.
- Use ¼" seam allowance for all stitching unless otherwise instructed.
- Use a short-to-medium stitch length.
- Make sure your seams are accurate.

Quilting Tools & Supplies
- Rotary cutter and mat
- Scissors for paper and fabric
- Non-slip quilting rulers
- Marking tools
- Sewing machine
- Sewing machine feet:
    ¼" seaming foot (for piecing)
    Walking or even-feed foot (for piecing or quilting)
    Darning or free-motion foot (for free-motion quilting)
- Quilting hand-sewing needles
- Straight pins
- Curved safety pins for basting
- Seam ripper
- Iron and ironing surface

Basic Techniques

Appliqué

Fusible Appliqué
All templates in *Quilter's World* are reversed for use with this technique.

1. Trace the instructed number of templates ¼" apart onto the paper side of paper-backed fusible web. Cut apart the templates, leaving a margin around each, and fuse to the wrong side of the fabric following fusible web manufacturer's instructions.

2. Cut the appliqué pieces out on the traced lines, remove paper backing and fuse to the background referring to the appliqué motif given.

3. Finish appliqué raw edges with a straight, satin, blanket, zigzag or blind-hem machine stitch with matching or invisible thread.

Turned-Edge Appliqué
1. Trace the printed reversed templates onto template plastic. Flip the template over and mark as the right side.

2. Position the template, right side up, on the right side of fabric and lightly trace, spacing images ½" apart. Cut apart, leaving a ¼" margin around the traced lines.

3. Clip curves and press edges ¼" to the wrong side around the appliqué shape.

4. Referring to the appliqué motif, pin or baste appliqué shapes to the background.

5. Hand-stitch shapes in place using a blind stitch and thread to match or machine-stitch using a short blind hemstitch and either matching or invisible thread.

Borders
Most *Quilter's World* patterns give an exact size to cut borders. You may check those sizes by comparing them to the horizontal and vertical center measurements of your quilt top.

Straight Borders
1. Mark the centers of the side borders and quilt top sides.

2. Stitch borders to quilt top sides with right sides together and matching raw edges and center marks using a ¼" seam. Press seams toward borders.

3. Repeat with top and bottom border lengths.

Mitered Borders
1. Add at least twice the border width to the border lengths instructed to cut.

2. Center and sew the side borders to the quilt, beginning and ending stitching ¼" from the quilt corner and backstitching (Figure 1). Repeat with the top and bottom borders.

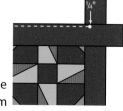

Figure 1

3. Fold and pin quilt right sides together at a 45-degree angle on one corner (Figure 2). Place a straightedge along the fold and lightly mark a line across the border ends.

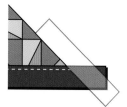

Figure 2

4. Stitch along the line, backstitching to secure. Trim seam to ¼" and press open (Figure 3).

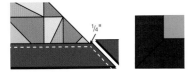

Figure 3

Quilt Backing & Batting

We suggest that you cut your backing and batting 8" larger than the finished quilt-top size. If preparing the backing from standard-width fabrics, remove the selvages and sew two or three lengths together; press seams open. If using 108"-wide fabric, trim to size on the straight grain of the fabric.

Prepare batting the same size as your backing. You can purchase prepackaged sizes or battings by the yard and trim to size.

Quilting

1. Press quilt top on both sides and trim all loose threads.

2. Make a quilt sandwich by layering the backing right side down, batting and quilt top centered right side up on flat surface and smooth out. Pin or baste layers together to hold.

3. Mark quilting design on quilt top and quilt as desired by hand or machine. *Note: If you are sending your quilt to a professional quilter, contact them for specifics about preparing your quilt for quilting.*

4. When quilting is complete, remove pins or basting. Trim batting and backing edges even with raw edges of quilt top.

Binding the Quilt

1. Join binding strips on short ends with diagonal seams to make one long strip; trim seams to ¼" and press seams open (Figure 4).

2. Fold 1" of one short end to wrong side and press. Fold the binding strip in half with wrong sides together along length, again referring to Figure 4; press.

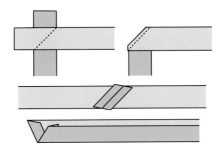

Figure 4

3. Starting about 3" from the folded short end, sew binding to quilt top edges, matching raw edges and using a ¼" seam. Stop stitching ¼" from corner and backstitch (Figure 5).

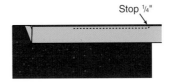

Stop ¼"

Figure 5

4. Fold binding up at a 45-degree angle to seam and then down even with quilt edges, forming a pleat at corner, referring to Figure 6.

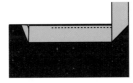

Figure 6

5. Resume stitching from corner edge as shown in Figure 6, down quilt side, backstitching ¼" from next corner. Repeat, mitering all corners, stitching to within 3" of starting point.

6. Trim binding end long enough to tuck inside starting end and complete stitching (Figure 7).

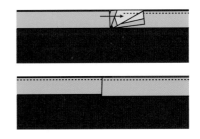

Figure 7

7. Fold binding to quilt back and stitch in place by hand or machine to complete your quilt.

Quilting Terms

- **Appliqué:** Adding fabric motifs to a foundation fabric by hand or machine (see Appliqué section of Basic Techniques).
- **Basting:** This temporarily secures layers of quilting materials together with safety pins, thread or a spray adhesive in preparation for quilting the layers.

  Use a long, straight stitch to hand- or machine-stitch one element to another holding the elements in place during construction and usually removed after construction.
- **Batting:** An insulating material made in a variety of fiber contents that is used between the quilt top and back to provide extra warmth and loft.
- **Binding:** A finishing strip of fabric sewn to the outer raw edges of a quilt to cover them.

  Straight-grain binding strips, cut on the crosswise straight grain of the fabric (see Straight & Bias Grain Lines illustration on page 62), are commonly used.

  Bias binding strips are cut at a 45-degree angle to the straight grain of the fabric. They are used when binding is being added to curved edges.

- **Block:** The basic quilting unit that is repeated to complete the quilt's design composition. Blocks can be pieced, appliquéd or solid and are usually square or rectangular in shape.
- **Border:** The frame of a quilt's central design used to visually complete the design and give the eye a place to rest.
- **Fabric Grain:** The fibers that run either parallel (lengthwise grain) or perpendicular (crosswise grain) to the fabric selvage are straight grain.

  Bias is any diagonal line between the lengthwise or crosswise grain. At these angles the fabric is less stable and stretches easily. The true bias of a woven fabric is a 45-degree angle between the lengthwise and crosswise grain lines.

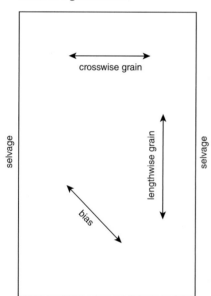

Straight & Bias Grain Lines

- **Mitered Corners:** Matching borders or turning bindings at a 45-degree angle at corners.
- **Patchwork:** A general term for the completed blocks or quilts that are made from smaller shapes sewn together.

- **Pattern:** This may refer to the design of a fabric or to the written instructions for a particular quilt design.
- **Piecing:** The act of sewing smaller pieces and/or units of a block or quilt together.

  Paper or foundation piecing is sewing fabric to a paper or cloth foundation in a certain order.

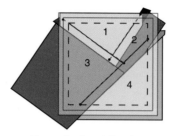

Foundation Piecing

String or chain piecing is sewing pieces together in a continuous string without clipping threads between sections.

String or Chain Piecing

- **Pressing:** Pressing is the process of placing the iron on the fabric, lifting it off the fabric and placing it down in another location to flatten seams or crease fabric without sliding the iron across the fabric.

  Quilters do not usually use steam when pressing, since it can easily distort fabric shapes.

  Generally, seam allowances are pressed toward the darker fabric in quilting so that they do not show through the lighter fabric.

  Seams are pressed in opposite directions where seams are being joined to allow seams to butt against each other and to distribute bulk.

Seams are pressed open when multiple seams come together in one place.

If you have a question about pressing direction, consult a comprehensive quilting guide for guidance.

- **Quilt (noun):** A sandwich of two layers of fabric with a third insulating material between them that is then stitched together with the edges covered or bound.
- **Quilt (verb):** Stitching several layers of fabric materials together with a decorative design. Stippling, crosshatch, channel, in-the-ditch, freemotion, allover and meandering are all terms for quilting designs.

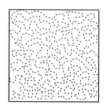 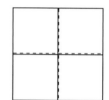

Meandering   **Stitch-in-the-ditch**

 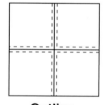

Channel   **Outline**

- **Quilt Sandwich:** A layer of insulating material between a quilt's top and back fabric.
- **Rotary Cutting:** Using a rotary cutting blade and straightedge to cut fabric.
- **Sashing:** Strips of fabric sewn between blocks to separate or set off the designs.
- **Subcut:** A second cutting of rotary-cut strips that makes the basic shapes used in block and quilt construction.
- **Template:** A pattern made from a sturdy material which is then used to cut shapes for patchwork and appliqué quilting.

Quilting Skill Levels

- **Beginner:** A quilter who has been introduced to the basics of cutting, piecing and assembling a quilt top and is working to master these skills. Someone who has the knowledge of how to sandwich, quilt and bind a quilt, but may not have necessarily accomplished the task yet.

- **Confident Beginner:** A quilter who has pieced and assembled several quilt tops and is comfortable with the process, and is now ready to move on to more challenging techniques and projects using at least two different techniques.

- **Intermediate:** A quilter who is comfortable with most quilting techniques and has a good understanding for design, color and the whole process. A quilter who is experienced in paper piecing, bias piecing and projects involving multiple techniques. Someone who is confident in making fabric selections other than those listed in the pattern.

- **Advanced:** A quilter who is looking for a challenging design. Someone who knows she or he can make any type of quilt. Someone who has the skills to read, comprehend and complete a pattern, and is willing to take on any technique. A quilter who is comfortable in her or his skills and has the ability to select fabric suited to the project. ●

Special Thanks

Please join us in thanking the talented designers
whose work is featured in this collection.

Holly Daniels
Flutter Pinwheels, page 43

Gina Gempesaw
A Quilter's Wreath, page 38
Turnstiles, page 3

Deb Karasik
Pinwheels With a Bite, page 31

Tricia Lynn Maloney
Pinwheel Baby, page 8

Jo Moury
Pinwheel Garden, page 48

Julie Weaver
Candy Kisses, page 15
Serenity, page 21

Supplies

We would like to thank the following manufacturers who provided
materials to our designers to make sample projects for this book.

Candy Kisses, page 15: Thermore® batting from Hobbs.

Flutter Pinwheels, page 43: Aloha Girl fabric collection
from Moda; Warm & White batting from The Warm
Company.

Pinwheel Baby, page 8: Good Natured fabric collection by
Riley Blake; Quilter's 80/20 batting from Fairfield.

Pinwheel Garden, page 48: Botanical Blue fabric collection
from Northcott; Bottom Line and Sew Fine thread from
Superior; quilted on HQ's Sweet 19.

Pinwheels With a Bite, page 31: Batiks by Hoffman of
California; thread from Superior; 80/20 batting from
Pellon. Pieced and quilted on a Brother Dreamweaver
Innovis VQ3000 sewing machine. Designed in EQ7.

Serenity, page 21: Bella Solid and True Luck fabric
collections from Moda; Thermore® batting from Hobbs.

Pretty Pinwheels is published by Annie's, 306 East Parr Road, Berne, IN 46711. Printed in USA. Copyright © 2015 Annie's. All rights reserved.
This publication may not be reproduced in part or in whole without written permission from the publisher.

RETAIL STORES: If you would like to carry this publication or any other Annie's publications, visit AnniesWSL.com.

Every effort has been made to ensure that the instructions in this publication are complete and accurate. We cannot, however, take responsibility for human error,
typographical mistakes or variations in individual work. Please visit AnniesCustomerService.com to check for pattern updates.

ISBN: 978-1-57367-904-6

1 2 3 4 5 6 7 8 9